POCKET PICTOR
Yorkshire

John Potter

MYRIAD
LONDON

Leeds The commercial and financial capital of Yorkshire and its largest city, Leeds has many fine buildings. Dominating the heart of the city is Leeds Town Hall, constructed between 1853-58 and designed by Hull architect Cuthbert Brodrick. This solid and imposing building is topped by a magnificent domed clocktower rising to 225ft (68m). The owl is a symbol of Leeds that also appears on the city's coat of arms. The County Arcade with Cross Arcade and the recently covered Queen Victoria Street constitute the City's Victoria Quarter – one of the most beautiful shopping environments in the north. The arcade has Siena marble columns and balustrades and an arched cast-iron roof.

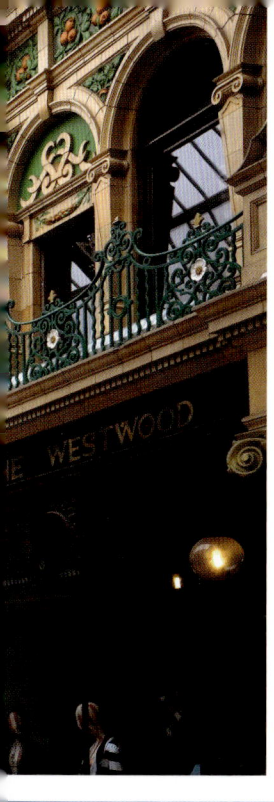

Modern Leeds New buildings are a hallmark of Leeds. Above is No 1 City Square, a 12-storey-block with black granite base. Leeds Waterfront was the city's historic dock area at the termini of the Aire and Calder Navigation and Leeds and Liverpool Canal. It has now been transformed by the conversion of old warehouses and the construction of apartments and offices.

Harewood House This magnificent country house (above), the home of Earl and Countess Lascelles, was built by the York architect John Carr between 1759 and 1772. The interiors were the work of Robert Adams and much furniture is by Robert Chippendale.
Pontefract The octagonal tower of St Giles' church (left).
Keighley Cliffe Castle Museum (right) is set amongst beautiful parkland.
Bradford The Alhambra Theatre (top right) was built in 1914 for the musical impresario Frank Laidler, the "King of Pantomime". The magnificent new Gothic Town Hall (far right) dates from 1873.

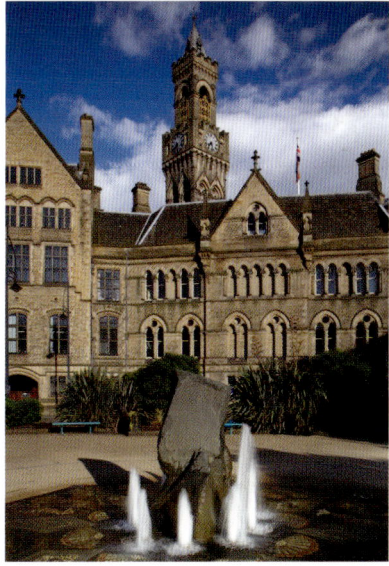

Halifax Built in a valley seven miles south-west of Bradford, Halifax is the capital of Calderdale. The town owes its prosperity to the wool trade and its town hall was designed by Sir Charles Barry, the architect of the Houses of Parliament. The Victoria Theatre (below), was built in 1901 originally as a concert hall and was converted into a theatre in 1960. The beautiful foyer contains a bust to Queen Victoria and a broad staircase surmounted by a beautiful stained-glass dome. The Wainhouse Tower (right) was built for John Edward Wainhouse to carry the smoke and fumes produced by his dye works out of the Calder valley.

Haworth The Brontë Parsonage Museum at Haworth (right) is a treasure trove of paintings, books and papers that belonged to the Brontës. The rooms have been lovingly restored to convey to visitors what life was like for the parson and his family of writers.

Huddersfield This West Riding town boasts 1,660 listed buildings – only Bristol and Westminster have more. One of the town's most famous sons was the prime minister Harold Wilson (1916-1995); his statue graces St George's Square.

Huddersfield Town Hall This magnificent building (above right) designed by John H Abbey, doubles as a concert hall and is home to the renowned Huddersfield Choral Society.

Hebden Bridge Eight miles west of Halifax, this beautiful town grew rapidly in the 18th and 19th centuries as a result of the wool trade.

Castle Hill The hill fort (above) at Almondbury near Huddersfield, seen here from Farnley Tyas, is made up of a series of Iron Age and medieval earthworks. The flat-topped hill has been the site of Chartist rallies as well as prize-fighting. The Victoria or Jubilee tower was added in 1899 to celebrate Queen Victoria's Diamond Jubilee two years earlier.

Holme Valley The Digley reservoir (above) is one of a number in the upper Holme valley overlooking Holmfirth. Immediately to the west is the smaller Bilberry reservoir which burst its banks in 1852, causing the death of 81 people.

Holmfirth Sid's Cafe (right) is just one of the Holmfirth locations used in the television series *Last of the Summer Wine*. This picturesque Pennine town developed rapidly in the 16th century thanks to the cloth industry and slate and stone mines.

Pateley Bridge The picturesque town of Pateley Bridge (right) was once a centre for leadmining and stone quarrying, both of which feature in the town's Nidderdale Museum, housed in the former workhouse opposite St Cuthbert's church. England's oldest sweetshop, established in 1827, is on the high street.

Middlesmoor Visitors to Middlesmoor can enjoy dramatic views down the valley towards the Gouthwaite reservoir from the old graveyard (below). Sited at the head of Nidderdale, the village clings to the top of a large hill, its stone cottages and cobbled streets huddled together to form a pretty hamlet cut off from the outside world.

Bolton Abbey This beautiful Augustinian priory (above) is an immense draw to visitors and an ever-popular picnic site. Further along the river lies "the Strid" – the narrow chasm through which the river Wharfe gushes in a thunderous and dramatic cascade.

Skipton The southern gateway to the Dales boasts an attractive stretch of the Leeds-Liverpool canal just a few minutes walk from the hustle and bustle of the busy high street. Skipton Castle (left) is one of the best preserved medieval castles in Britain.

Appletreewick Four miles south-east of Grassington, this peaceful Wharfedale village rests on a steep slope overlooked by the craggy summit of Simon's Seat.

Linton Situated seven miles north of Skipton, the stone cottages of this characterful village (right) cluster around the village green which slopes down towards Linton Beck. Along the beck are waterfalls, a weir, a packhorse bridge and the delightful St Michael's church.

Grassington Standing at the point where two historically important roads cross in the dale, Grassington (below) is the largest settlement in upper Wharfedale. The town has a beautiful cobbled market square with an ornate water pump.

Malhamdale The area around Malham is famous for its limestone scenery, particularly Malham Cove — the 250ft high rockface which stands just behind the village.
Just a few miles north-east of Malham is the dramatic limestone ravine of Gordale Scar, which has inspired poets and painters for hundreds of years.

Hubberholme Named after a Viking chieftain, Hubberholme is located on the Dales Way four and a half miles from Kettlewell. It is famous for the beautiful church of St Michael whose choir stalls and pews were constructed by Robert Thompson, the "mouse man" of Kilburn whose trademark – a carved mouse – is found on his work.

Arncliffe The pretty hamlet of Arncliffe lies at the heart of beautiful secluded Littondale. Littondale was the setting for part of Charles Kingsley's novel *The Water Babies*, and it was also chosen originally as the setting for the popular long-running television series *Emmerdale*.

Howgill Fells Close to the town of Sedbergh, these distinctive rounded hills mark the point where the more gentle fells of the north-west Dales meet the higher mountains of south-east Cumbria.

Brigflatts The Quaker Friends Meeting House at Brigflatts, half a mile from Sedbergh, was built in 1675 when the village was a thriving and largely self-sufficient community.

Dentdale With its white-painted houses and softly rounded fells, Dentdale shares many characteristics with the Lake District. The pretty village of Dent is actually in Cumbria, four miles south-east of Sedbergh, although it lies within the Yorkshire Dales National Park. Linking Dentdale with Ribblesdale to the south is the beautiful Settle to Carlisle railway line, one of the most scenic rail routes in Europe. Dent station lies four miles from the village and is the highest mainline railway station in Britain. Close by are the Arten Gill and Dent Head viaducts, two of the most spectacular constructions on any railway line in Britain.

Hawes Known as the "little capital" of Upper Wensleydale, Hawes is Yorkshire's highest market town. The town houses the Wensleydale Creamery where the famous Wensleydale cheese, first made by local monks, is now produced.

Wensleydale This broad fertile dale (seen to the right near Hawes in early winter) cuts through the northern part of the region. At its heart is the river Ure with its many waterfalls such as those at West Burton and Aysgarth.

Askrigg Just one mile north-east of Bainbridge on the northern side of Wensleydale, this tiny settlement is best known as the setting for the popular television series *All Creatures Great and Small*. Above the village sits Askrigg Common and beyond it is the distinctive form of Addlebrough.

Gayle North of Hawes, Gayle is sited at the foot of Sleddale. Duerley Beck cascades over a series of limestone steps in the centre of the village before rushing below a packhorse bridge.

Bainbridge Set in the heart of Wensleydale, Bainbridge (above), has a wide and sweeping village green with ancient village stocks and mature trees. It is overlooked from the east by the remains of an unexcavated Roman settlement.

West Burton West Burton Falls (left) is a popular location for artists and photographers. Situated to the east of the village, the falls are easily reached on foot. The upper fall was featured in the film *Robin Hood, Prince of Thieves* starring Kevin Costner in the title role.

Middleham Just two miles south of Leyburn, Middleham Castle was built around 1170 by Robert Fitz Randolph during the reign of Henry II. The keep has 12ft (3.5m) thick walls and is one of the largest in England.

Castle Bolton The small village of Castle Bolton, five miles west of Leyburn, is dominated by Bolton Castle (left). This massive fortress has been a feature of the Wensleydale landscape since 1379. It is one of the country's best preserved castles. Mary Queen of Scots was imprisoned here during 1568 and 1569. Two of the castle gardens, the Herb Garden and the Walled Garden, have been restored along medieval lines providing visitors with a beautiful setting and wonderful views of the dale.

Gunnerside Surrounded by stunning windswept fells, this unspoiled picturesque settlement (above) sits at the foot of Gunnerside Gill. The valley bottoms are dotted with attractive field barns and drystone walls.

Richmond The capital of Swaledale, Richmond (left and below) is dominated by its castle keep, part of the massive fortification built by Alan the Red of Brittany, a trusted supporter of William I. Richmond ranks among the most beautiful towns in England, with many elegant Georgian houses, cobbled streets and pretty cottage gardens.

Muker The pretty village of Muker (left) sits proudly above Straw Beck just before it joins the river Swale about one mile east of Thwaite.

Reeth Situated 12 miles west of Richmond, Reeth has a spacious, triangular village green which provides stunning views of the surrounding Swaledale countryside. The village was once a centre for both lead-mining and knitting, and now continues to be the market town for the local area.

Fountains Abbey One of the most popular attractions in Yorkshire, Fountains Abbey (right) and Studley Royal is a huge estate which includes the largest abbey ruins in England, a spectacular Georgian water garden and deer park.

Jervaulx The beautiful ruins of this Cistercian abbey (below) lie between Masham and Leyburn.

Masham The attractive small town of Masham (left) has a cobbled marketplace surrounded by elegant Georgian houses, stone cottages, shops and tearooms. The spire of St Mary's overlooks the town centre. The Masham Steam Engine and Fair Organ Rally is a spectacular event which takes place every July.

Ripon The gateway to the eastern Dales, this cathedral city stands on the banks of the river Ure. The city has three unusual museums – the Courthouse, the Prison Museum and the Workhouse Museum. An attractive canal, linking Ripon via the river Ouse to the Humber, lies to the south of the city.

Knaresborough This beautiful town (above) grew up around the steep sides of the gorge of the river Nidd. The town's Norman castle (left) was used as a hideout by the four knights who murdered Thomas à Beckett in 1170. The castle was badly damaged during the Civil War when Parliamentarians beseiged the town.

Castle Howard Set amongst magnificent parkland north-east of York, Castle Howard is one of Britain's finest historic houses. It gained fame with television audiences in 1981 when it was used as the setting for *Brideshead Revisited*.

Harrogate Bettys & Taylors opened their first "continental-style tea room" (right) on Parliament Street, overlooking Montpellier Gardens, in 1919. The Royal Pump Room (below) is a reminder of Harrogate's spa heritage.

York The largest Gothic cathedral in northern Europe, York Minster (right) is the seat of the archbishop of York, the second highest office in the Church of England. There has been a church here since 627; work on the current Minster began in 1220 and was not completed until 1472. York Minster is famous for the Great East window, completed in 1408, the largest expanse of medieval stained glass in the world. The view above looks up to the ceiling of the Transept Tower.

York Abbey The ruins of St Mary's Abbey (left) lie to the west of the Minster in the Yorkshire Museum gardens. The Benedictine Abbey was founded in 1055 and became one of the richest religious settlements in the north of England. In 1539 the monastic community was disbanded and the abbey destroyed during the Dissolution.

River Ouse York's historic Mansion House on the banks of the Ouse was built in the 15th century. The building served as a meeting place for the guilds of York who controlled trade within the city.

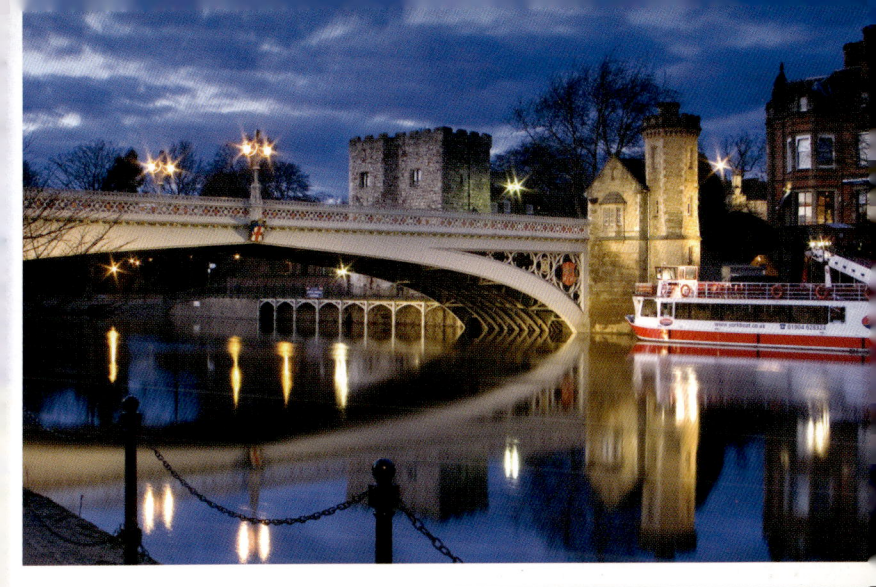

Lendal Bridge This elegant iron bridge with stone towers at either end was built by Thomas Page in 1863. It is one of nine bridges over the river Ouse in York.

The Shambles One of the highlights of this beautiful city, this meandering medieval street leads up to the Minster. Today it is filled with charming shops; in the Middle Ages it was home to many butchers. Its name is derived from the Anglo-Saxon word *shammels* – meaning an open-air slaughterhouse. The Shambles is so narrow that some of the upper floors of the houses are within touching distance of those on the opposite side of the street.

Pickering This elegant market town is located on the southern edge of the North York Moors. In the centre of the town is Beck Isle Museum of Rural Life, housed in a Grade 2 listed Regency mansion.

Thirsk Overlooking the Hambleton Hills, the lively town of Thirsk hosts a twice-weekly open-air market. James Herriot, the author of the semi-biographical novels *All Creatures Great and Small*, was a vet in the town; his house is open to the public.

Rosedale The long, extended valley of Rosedale stretches out in a south-easterly direction from Westerdale Moor and Danby High Moor towards Hartoft End and Cropton Forest.

Mallyan Spout
The highest waterfall on the North York Moors, Mallyan Spout, near Goathland, cascades 60ft down the side of West Beck Gorge. A short walk alongside the beck to the right of the Mallyan Spout Hotel leads to the picturesque waterfall.

Farndale The tiny and picturesque hamlet of Church Houses nestles between the mighty Rudland Rigg and Blakey Ridge in glorious scenery at the heart of much-loved Farndale.

Helmsley This is one of the most attractive country towns in North Yorkshire. A pretty stream runs through the town at the back of the market square with a quaint stone bridge.

Rievaulx Abbey This 13th-century church is reputed to have been one of the finest monastic churches in northern Britain. Like all Cistercian monasteries it was deliberately secluded from the outside world. The site of Rievaulx, in the depths of the narrow Rye valley, must have provided the monks with a haven of solitude.

Staithes Known locally as "Steers", meaning "landing place", Staithes has a dramatic setting on the rugged stretch of coast north of Whitby. The town's white-painted cottages are perched haphazardly on any available space. Staithes has attracted many artists over the years; in the late 1890s the so-called Staithes Group of around 30 artists were active in the area.

Robin Hood's Bay The pretty fishing village of Robin Hood's Bay has steep winding streets lined with old houses and cottages. Cobbled ginnels or alleyways thread their way between the houses. The bay is seen here from the coastal footpath with the town in the distance and the cliffs of Bay Ness behind. The Coast to Coast trail ends here.

Whitby The seaside town of Whitby is where the young James Cook learned the seafarer's trade. In 1746 he took up residence with John Walker in an elegant 17th-century harbourside house in Grape Lane; the house is now the splendid Captain Cook Memorial Museum. Whitby's skyline is dominated by the ruins of St Hilda's Abbey, high up on East Cliff. Next to the abbey is the church of St Mary.

Scarborough The ruined Norman castle and its headland dominate Scarborough's skyline. The headland stands 150ft (46m) above the harbour and, as can be seen in the photograph, on a clear day a fantastic view can be enjoyed from Oliver's Mount. The Spa Complex, with its superb parks, gardens, theatres and conference hall sits majestically beside the principal bathing beach.

Flamborough The coastline at Flamborough is magnificent with sheltered shingle coves fronting the sea backed by cliffs, sea caves and dramatic stacks. Bempton has some of the highest cliffs on the east coast of Britain, and is famous as a seabird nature reserve, featuring the only gannet colony in mainland Britain.

Bridlington This popular resort has two glorious long sandy beaches, miles of elegant promenades and a very pretty and bustling harbour. Flamborough Head and its distinctive lighthouse are clearly visible from the north pier. Bridlington is divided into two areas: the old town, which lies about a mile inland and Bridlington quay.

Spurn Point Situated on the north bank of the entrance to the river Humber, Spurn Point is a beautiful and unique place. The three-mile long finger of land that snakes out into the Humber estuary is constantly being reshaped by coastal erosion. Spurn Bird Observatory was opened to visitors in 1946 and provides birdwatchers with an ideal location to observe bird migration.

The Deep The gleaming glass and aluminium marine life centre called The Deep opened in 2002. It stands at the confluence of the rivers Hull and Humber and is part of the vision of regeneration for Hull.

Humber Bridge Opened in 1981, the Humber Bridge links north Lincolnshire and Yorkshire. Industry and businesses in towns such as Immingham and Grimsby have benefited from a link to the port of Hull and motorway connections to Manchester, Leeds and Liverpool.

Beverley This ancient town, eight miles north of Hull, has held a large market since medieval times. The beautiful parish church of St John and St Martin (below left), generally known as Beverley Minster, is regarded as one of the most impressive Gothic buildings in Europe.

Wentworth Woodhouse This magnificent mansion stands close to the village of Wentworth. Its East or Palladian front is the longest frontage of any house in Europe.

Conisbrough Castle This magnificent stone castle (right) stands above an important crossing point on the river Don. Its massive cylindrical keep dominates the surrounding countryside.

Roche Abbey The peaceful ruins (left) of this former Cistercian abbey lie nine miles from Doncaster and are now in the care of English Heritage.

Cusworth Hall This Palladian-style country house (below) stands in a landscaped park two miles north of Doncaster.

Barnsley Sited at the junction of Church Street and Shambles Street at the top of Market Hill, Barnsley Town Hall (right) was erected when Barnsley was still the coal capital of South Yorkshire; its limestone tower still dominates the townscape today.

Stainborough Castle

The recently renovated mock medieval castle (below) is in the grounds of Wentworth Castle, at Stainborough. The beautiful 60-acre Castle Gardens with over 500 acres of parkland and woodland walks are rated as one of the finest landscaped amenities in the county. The hall is now Northern College, an adult education centre.

Sheffield Crowds enjoy a sunny summer's day in Sheffield's Peace Garden (above), a green space right in the heart of the city in front of the town hall. The low curved roof of the city's Winter Garden, a temperate glasshouse, can be seen on the far right. The Town Hall which stands at the junction of Surrey Street and Pinstone Street was built of Derbyshire sandstone in 1897. The high street (left) leads from the site of the castle and the market area towards the cathedral. In the distance is Kelmsley House, the Sheffield Telegraph building and in the foreground the former John Walsh's department store which was rebuilt following bomb damage in the second world war.

Blakey Ridge Bronze Age burial mounds and lonely prehistoric standing stones abound on the Lyke Wake Walk, a long-distance footpath which traverses the North Yorks Moors.